100 Inspirational Quotes & Floral Bookmarks to Print and Color

Copyright ©2020 Niki McNeil

All rights reserved. No part of this publication may be reproduced, distributed, or transmitted in any form or by any means, including photocopying, recording, or other electronic or mechanical methods, without the prior written permission of the publisher, except in the case of brief quotations embodied in reviews and certain other noncommercial uses permitted by copyright law.

Published August 2020 by Niki McNeil

Written and Illustrated by Niki McNeil

The What & The Why:

This book is the culmination of my first 100 Day Project. This concept popped up during one of my countless hours of mindless web scrolling near the beginning of the Covid-19 lockdown. Given that the biggest goal of a 100 day project is to create daily for 100 days, I knew I was **all in** as I had recently myself to the concept of creating more and consuming less. I went through the process of brainstorming what I was good at, what I loved doing, what I wanted to do more of, and what I dreamed of doing in my lifetime, as well as the basics of why did I really want to do this, how much time I had to commit, and how would I keep myself accountable. In the end, for my first project, I decided to combine my love of quotes with my desire to learn to draw flowers better – and what better format than a bookmark?! Through sharing my daily bookmark I had many friends and family ask if I'd be selling them when I was done. I had not thought that far in advance, I was just doing something I enjoyed and keeping my mind sane during a turbulent time. Ultimately, I decided to combine them all into the book you see here. The quotes were chosen daily based on my moods; you'll see on days 16-18 there are 2 bookmarks for each day. This is because my initial quote pick had a negative tone, as I was not in a great place, but after reflection on the first finished bookmark I decided I wanted to come up with a way to "reframe" my first one, so I kept that theme for the set of 3. It was thought provoking to realize that sometimes it really is how you look at something that determines how you will react. I left the blank templates after day 100 as I thought you might like to give a try at designing a bookmark or two yourself.

The How:
Because I am unable to dictate which paper this book is printed on when using Amazon's self-publishing, I suggest you print your own on a high quality cardstock using the free download link provided at the end of the book. This allows you to make multiple copies/prints of your favorite bookmarks as gifts and use this book as a visual catalog of what to color next. The book is single sided to allow you to color and cut directly from the book if you desire.
Spice them up a bit by mounting on fun scrapbook paper or colorful cardstock; the possibilities are endless for how fancy you want to make them! You can even hole punch the top and add ribbon if you would like.

What's Next?
Follow EclecticallyMeNiki on Facebook/Pinterest/Instagram to see what my next 100 Day Project will be.

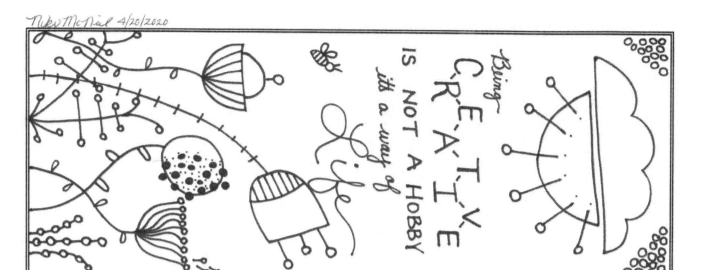

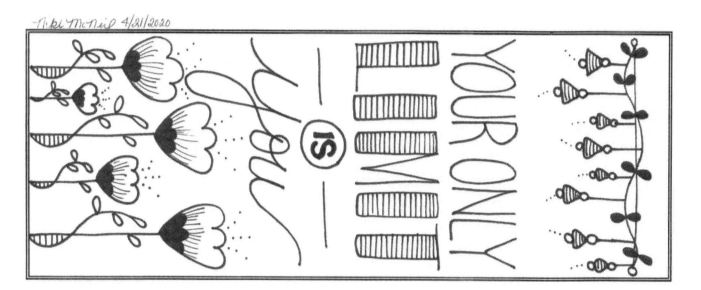

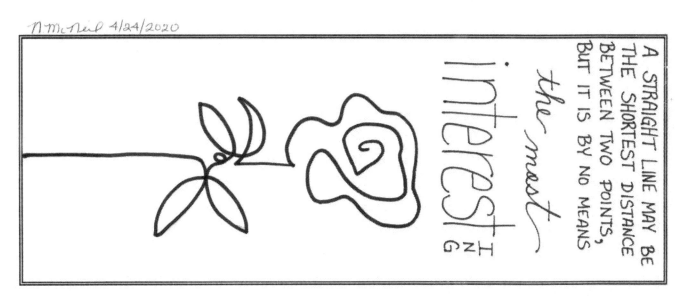

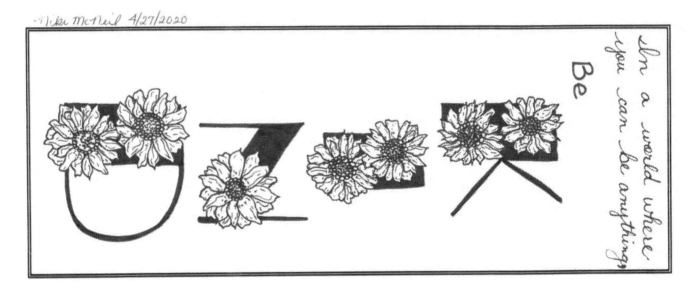

Niki McNeil 4/29/2020

Niki McNeil 4/30/2020

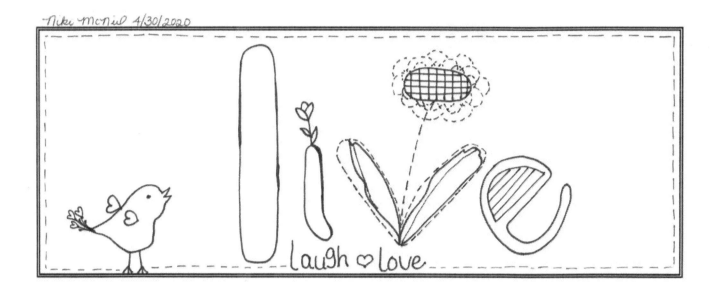

Niki McNeil 5/1/2020

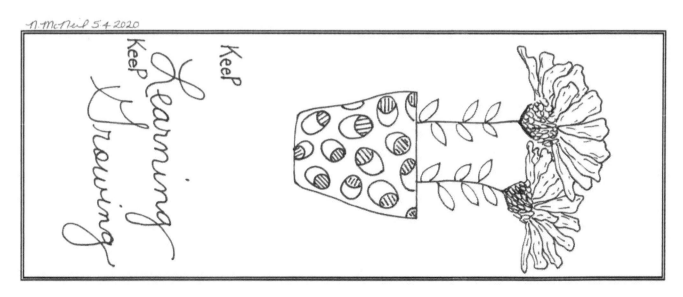

n.mcneil 5/5/2020

Just because someone carries it well doesn't mean it isn't HEAVY

n.mcneil 5/6/2020

Sometimes all you can do is lie in bed, and hope to fall asleep before you fall APART

n.mcneil 5/7/2020

The biggest communication problem is we do not listen to understand We listen to respond

n.mcneil 5/11/2020

Reading gives us someplace to go when we have to stay where we are.
— mason cooley

n.mcneil 5/12/2020

Life is short, read fast

n.mcneil 5/13/2020

From little seeds, grow mighty dreams

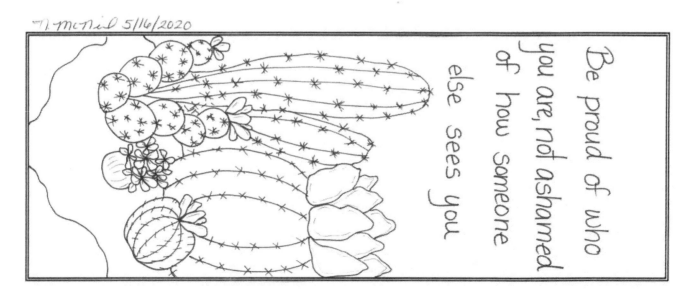

n. McNeil 5/23/2020

IF IT DOESN'T Challenge you IT WON'T Change you

n. McNeil 5/24/2020

You're a Limited Edition

n. McNeil 5/25/2020

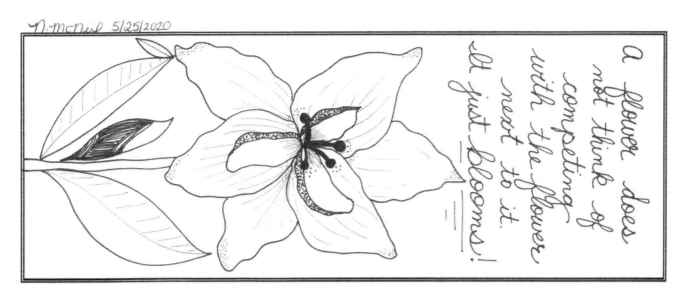

A flower does not think of competing with the flower next to it. It just blooms!

n.McNeil 5/26/2020

The meaning of life is to find your gift

The purpose of life is to give it away
—Pablo Picasso

n.McNeil 5/27/2020

Every time I judge someone else, I reveal an unhealed part of myself

n.McNeil 5/28/2020

Hope smiles from the threshold of the year to come, whispering, "It will be Happier..."
—Alfred Tennyson

n.mcNeil 5/29/2020

Boundaries are the distance at which I can love you and me simultaneously
- Prentis Hemphill

n.mcNeil 5/30/2020

Trade your expectations for appreciation, and your whole world changes instantly.

n.McNeil 5/31/2020

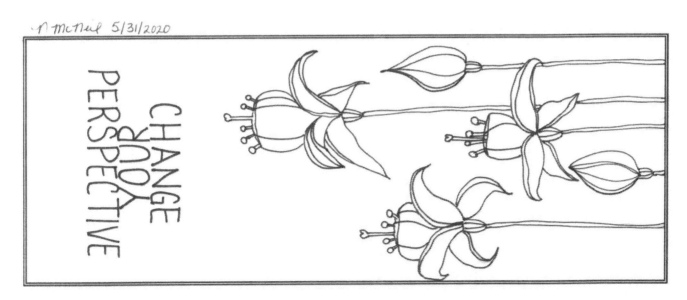

CHANGE YOUR PERSPECTIVE

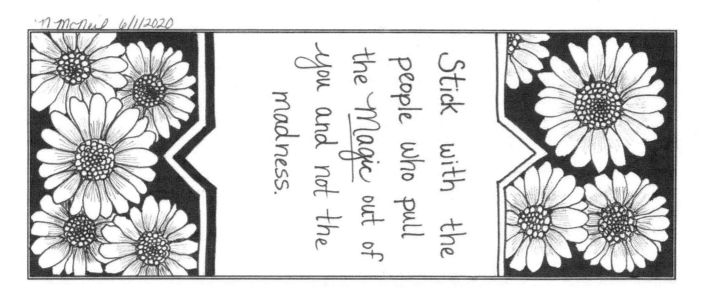

Stick with the people who pull the _Magic_ out of you and not the madness.

If you have the _power_ to make someone _happy_, do it! The world needs more of that.

Be Fearlessly Authentic

n. McNeil 6/4/2020

If everything around you seems dark. Look again, you may be the light. -Rumi

n. McNeil 6/5/2020

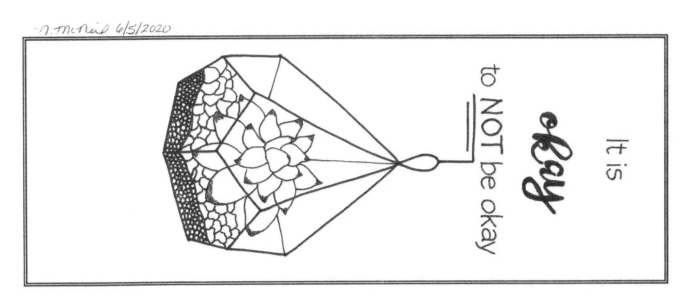

It is *okay* to NOT be okay

n. McNeil 6/6/2020

Stay in your own lane. Comparison kills creativity & joy -brene brown

n.mcneil 6/10/2020

n.mcneil 6/11/2020

n.mcneil 6/12/2020

n.mcneil 6/13/2020

The struggle you're in today is developing the strength you need for tomorrow.
—Robert Tew

n.mcneil 6/14/2020

It always seems impossible until it's done.
—Nelson Mandela

n.mcneil 6/15/2020

We don't GROW when things are easy; we GROW when we face challenges.

n. mcneil 6/16/2020

When things change inside you

things change around you

n. mcneil 6/17/2020

You fall in love with people who make you love

the person you are when you're around them.

n. mcneil 6/18/2020

believe IN YOURSELF

n. mcneil 6/19/2020

n. mcneil 6/20/2020

n. mcneil 6/21/2020

n. McNeil 6/25/2020

You are always one decision away from a totally different life.

n. McNeil 6/26/2020

Self care is how you take your power back

n. McNeil 6/27/2020

Courage above FEAR

n. McNeil 6/28/2020

Appreciate what you have, before time makes you appreciate what you had.

n. McNeil 6/29/2020

Love her... but leave her wild

n. McNeil 6/30/2020

Live like someone left the gate open

n.mcneil 7/1/2020

n.mcneil 7/2/2020

n.mcneil 7/3/2020

n. McNeil 7/4/2020

n. McNeil 7/5/2020

n. McNeil 7/6/2020

n.mcneil 7/7/2020

Your thoughts are powerful. Choose wisely!

n.mcneil 7/8/2020

Be bold enough to use your voice, brave enough to listen to your heart, and strong enough to live the life you've always imagined.

n.mcneil 7/9/2020

Do less Be more

n.mcneil 7/13/2020

— Ferris Bueller's Day Off

Life moves pretty fast. If you don't stop and look around once in a while, you could miss it.

n.mcneil 7/14/2020

Breathe, darling. This is just a chapter, not your whole story.

— S.C. Lourie

n.mcneil 7/15/2020

Be the reason someone smiles today.

n. mcneil 7/14/2020

Water your roots, so your *soul* can blossom

n. mcneil 7/17/2020

Keep your face towards the Sunshine and the shadows will fall behind you

n. mcneil 7/18/2020

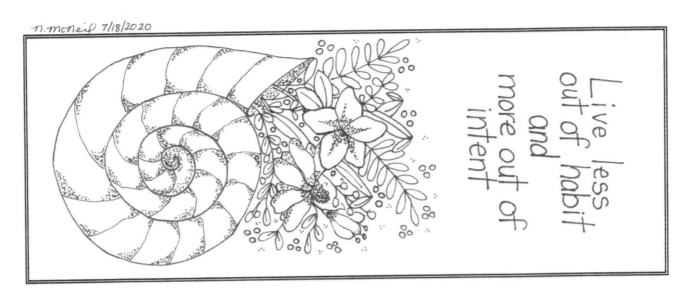

Live less out of habit and more out of intent

n.moneid 7/19/2020

Design a Life you Love

n.moneid 7/20/2020

never assume
never expect
just hope

n.moneid 7/21/2020

It is in your hands to make of our world a better one for all.
—Nelson Mandela

n. mcneil 7/22/2020

Believe in yourself and you will be Unstoppable

n. mcneil 7/23/2020

Life isn't about finding yourself. Life is about creating yourself.
— George Shaw

n. mcneil 7/24/2020

Keep taking time for yourself until you're you again
— Lalah Delia

n.mcneil 7/25/2020

We rise by lifting others

n.mcneil 7/26/2020

Tell the negative committee that meets inside your head to sit down and hush up!

n.mcneil 7/27/2020

Be Brave

n. McNeil 7/28/2020

I'm not telling you it's going to be easy, I'm telling you it's going to be worth it.

To download the free PDF of this book for ease of printing please visit

https://www.eclecticallymeniki.com/100-days-of-bookmarks-downloads

All images are copyrighted and may NOT be shared with anyone. The original purchaser may color and gift the bookmarks but images must be altered to be gifted, do not simply print out and gift as that is against the copyright.

Printed in Great Britain
by Amazon